"Adisa in the Ray of Sun"

BY

FOLORUNSHO AHMED ADEKUNLE

Copyright © (Folorunsho Ahmed Adekunle)

All rights reserved. No part of this publication may be reproduced, distributed, or transmitted in any form or by any means, including photocopying, recording, or other electronic or mechanical methods, without the prior written permission of the publisher, except in the case of brief quotations embodied in critical reviews and certain other non-commercial uses permitted by copyright law.

Author: Folorunsho Ahmed Adekunle

Editor: Eraita Oribhabor

ISBN (Paperback): 978-1-917267-34-2

Published by Nubian Republic on behalf of Palmwine Publishing Limited Nigeria

Email: info@palmwinepublishing.com

Address- UK: 86-90, Paul Street, London EC2A 4NE

Address- Nigeria: 1A Jos Road Bukuru, Plateau State, Nigeria.

www.palmwine publishing.com
www.raffiapress.com
www.nuciferaanalysis.com

DEDICATION

This Poetry Collection is dedicated to all teenagers in Africa who are being denied the opportunity of being motivated towards promoting their love for poetry and writing as career pathway.

ACKNOWLEDGMENT

'Trauma Of The Pierce' was first published on Amazon as E-book

'Podium Of Anxiety' was first published by Outside The Box Poetry Magazine

'The Aguero's Moment' was first published in Issue 4 of Waves Of Words Literary Magazine

Adisa In the Ray Of Sun - Folorunsho Ahmed Adekunle

Table of Contents

POEMS	PAGES
TITLE PAGE	
PUBLICATION PAGE	II
DEDICATION PAGE	III
ACKNOWLEDGMENT	1V
TABLE OF CONTENT	V
TABLE OF CONTENT	VI

THE POET AND HIS TRANCE
ADISA AND HIS WORDS	1
WRITE TO RIGHT	2
I WON'T FORGET MY HOME	3
SOMEDAY I WILL RECREATE	4
WORLD POETRY DAY	5

GAMBLING ADDICTION
DRAINING BET SHOP	6

RACISM AND NEO-COLONIALISM
KNEEL OF HYPOCRITES	8
LET MY PEOPLE GO	9
NEITHER BABA-IYABO	10

SEXUAL ABUSE
BRIDE AHEAD OF TIME	11
TRAUMA OF THE PIERCE	13
BEHIND SHADOW OF RAPE	14

BONDED BY THE SOIL
NATION WITH NO DESTINATION	16
UNITY IN DIVERSITY	18

ARTS, CULTURE AND THE ABUSE
MUSIC IS LIFE	19
THE THESPIANS	20
BEYOND THE PALMWINE	22
OJUDE OBA	24
HEINOUS TRIBAL MARK	25

UNDERPRIVILEGED WISHES
CHRISTMAS NOT MERRY	26
TABLE MANNER	27

DIRGE AND EXILE
JOURNEY OF COMMON DESTINATION	28
GRAVE LOVE	29
IMOLE	30
AFRIKA LIVES ON	31

FAITH AND RELIGION

GOD IS EVERYWHERE	32
THE AGUERO'S MOMENT	33

ROMANCE POETRY

MY MỌREMÍ ÀJÀSORÒ	34
LOVE PRICE	35
BE LIKE ZAINAB	36
SONNET FROM MY HEART	37

GEN-Z; SEXUAL IMMORALITY TRENDS

KOPA WAA KOPA WEE-MEN	38
WEATHER FOR TWO	39
THE BODY COUNT COUNTS	40
TRAUMA OF MASTURBATION	41
SILHOUETTE IN THE DARK	43

CHILD RIGHT TO EDUCATION

THE UNPRIVILEGED GRADUATE	45
THE DAY IN GOWN	47
SCHOOL GATE FOREST	49

MENTAL HEALTH AND DEPRESSION

STIFLE THE SUICIDE	51
BEHIND THE "HAPPY FAMILY	53
PODIUM OF ANXIETY	55

STATE OF NATION

TALIBANS AT OUR BACKYARD	56
SIX NINE	58
SNAKES ON LEGAL TENDER	59
THE HEN THE ROPE	60

FUNDAMENTAL HUMAN RIGHTS ADVOCACY

THE MESSENGER OF OUR PLIGHTS	61
AUTHORIZED CRIMINALS	62

HEALTH AND FOOD CONSUMPTION

THE KIDNEY OF THE COUNTRY	63

HUMOROUS POETRY

MAN' UNITED	65
ADISA THE TAILOR	66

ADISA AND HIS WORDS

Why did you choose to be a Poet?
With aroma of words beneath,
Taking their Emotion's breath,
Yet, like Karl Marx of zero wealth.

Where is Wole Soyinka's Bugatti?
They asked, in downcast curiosity.
Like Achebe's pocket entity,
Do you want to fall Apart in poverty?

With your fingers of fruitless flattery
Serving as enslaved Pen guards,
See your mates, Pablo and Barnabas,
Raining cash in party of Desert ballers.

Like words of piercing bullets,
Out rightly daring, killing my soul
What more can I say? Painfully fuming…
The dreams, I must continue navigating.

Poets in Trenches of the day,
Someday in great faith of payday,
Above the brown roofs I shall fly, someday,
Remember Adisa, and his words of today.

WRITE TO RIGHT

Lonely is him;–
A teen of a world I know,
His descendents came without his consent;
To the Soil of absent joy
And presence of unmatched fingers.

Innocent is him; a teen of no lust,
With Dreams, yielding no interest in dream-bank,
With a micro skull of wisdom,
Documenting lots day and night
Deeds of his destined world.

He lost his sleep, not his words,
The blazing Pen - his harmless weapon,
He fights to write to right,
Maybe, his words are heavy, maybe –
But his passion rendered all threats empty,
Truth couldn't set his blazers ablaze –
Neither free.

Every drop of ink is a word of freedom,
Seized not, to pen your plights,
In language of your diverse choice,
On a dark leaf, light was unveiled.

O' ye Teen!
Writing warrior of the world,
Take the course of the wise
With a broken heart,
Devoid of broken courage.
This is your call,
Continue writing to right.

I WON'T FORGET MY HOME

I won't forget my home
Where we cry oceans of tears
For people who passed away in cold,
But we want them to kick the bucket.

Home, my home…
Survival; the heart of our matter,
Struggle; grey hair of younger folks,
We drink from the pools of our sweat gutter.

Bad was the day lobbying for help,
Bullets of words spilled at us,
Draining the lake of our self-esteem,
Tears surely dehydrates, so we wept!

I won't forget my home, never!
When education finally made me
- A walking dictionary and impactful icon,
When I finally become a shining star,
I will come back home, as shinning blessing.

SOMEDAY, I WILL RECREATE

Someday! Someday!!
Someday, I will say…
Someday, I will recreate,
And piece through hates like a sword and be great.

Someday, I will find my un-missing lover,
My own loyal Michelle Obama,
The black-skinned, white-teethed lover,
The lady with a universe of ideas planted in her.

A lady of peace valley,
Never the heart-piecing baddie,
Presentable First Lady with "presence" of vibrancy!
Outspoken in her words to humanity.

We will drill through hard times,
And banish failure to Sambisa of our time,
Come rain, come shine, leaving shall be a crime.
And every home, a roof of happiness and good times!

Someday, I will say…
Like I promised my mother,
To be a good father,
Pride for my woman - No other!
In ocean of joy, my kids will say: "oh that's my father!"

Someday, I will recreate and be louder!
I will walk through aisle like Obama.
With my beautiful Michelle, like a winner.
Someday, I will be a conqueror! And my past won't matter.

WORLD POETRY DAY

The sick world lies helplessly
In a ward of words that could
Birth war or peace.
Poetry watches with blind eyes
From high hills of heavenly ways -
Bards heal the world
With therapeutic words.

DRAINING BET SHOP

A draining bet shop;
As quick as speed of light,
Fast results; no returns,
A pastry set of fixed scores,
Stationed in their system – displayed by monitor.

A draining bet shop;
One, two, nine, ten; all draw,
Sexy looking big odds, ready to drag
One into the pit of Lazarus,
Oh no! My stakes gone, wrong.

A draining bet shop;
A small length blocks,
Producing hell, in summer,
Army of pundits and gamblers,
Stuck indoor as captive bookies.

A draining bet shop;
Family men leave before dawn,
Nothing left on the dining table,
Virtual! Virtual!! Virtual!!!
The jobless youth's job insight.

A draining bet shop
Of paper flooded floor,
Tickets to heaven of bankruptcy,
Some with echoing bank rooms;
Have nothing, but lots to loose.

A draining bet shop;
Who knows your wrath?
Oh yeh Seekers of fast wealth;
In jiffy, a place they do not work;
Dear visual sport bet shop, drain no more.

KNEEL OF HYPOCRITES

The brutal knee of a white angel guard,
He piles the road of devil's throat in his backyard,
He stood on business of superior master's world,
And choke a creation with colours of the devil's skin.

The town showed no shock, for it's their norm,
Reminisce about the Caribbean's blacks sold in dust,
George Floyd floods the world like sand of the sea,
The sea bears bosom to the moon as seen.

Freely they watch his last breathe
As his soul flies high to the sky beneath,
A series we see often in cinemas,
When the United Nations is camera short.

They lie about his kneels,
The black lives' neck lives under their heels,
They sell the gospel of: "one people different colours"
Yet, George was taken in cold blood by skin color judge.

Humans can lean on humanity, so I heard
How long shall kneel be knead?
And, racism will be made to suffer and stutter,
Till then, continue to chant, black lives matters!

LET MY PEOPLE GO

I have seen eyes glued to the screen,
I have seen tears soak the cushion;
The party of Goosebumps in a mansion of clans,
Celebrating the cast and conquer of villains.

But here is my hero of high doughty,
Tho' he lost his cap in service of humanity,
Not all heroes wear caps anyways,
But on him a crown of clap is every day worn.

The piercing rod of his letter mail,
Patting way for educational bail,
"Let my people go" he wails,
Olumuyiwa Igbalajobi; the treasury hails.

Our masters are blinded to their colonies,
Our teachers denied their teachings,
Who could have thought they never taught us?
But Dr. Muyiwa says, we never lost all the balls.

NEITHER BABA-IYABO

Just take a look and deduce,
With eyes blind you use;
Reading the culture of The Duke,
Inhaling the mess of his book.

In shame, the shipped product,
Of his ways you bought,
And dump yours cheaply,
In party of his soothing lullaby.

Wake up! Oh thou Africans!
Blaze the edges of your Kampala,
Reclaim your birthright
In high pride of Mountain's height!

Shall I be made inferior
Without my consent that is superior?
It can never be me! Neither Baba-Iyabo;
The global Ambassador of our fading Culture.

BRIDE AHEAD OF TIME

I was growing,
And rising like stars of Dakar,
Imbedded by dreams,
A promising infant teenager I am.

Shortly as a teen;
Tubas and silver took my place
- In my father's house.
Garment of my sugary eyes was stripped off,
A denial of privilege of the best legacy.

I sobered without falling tears,
Like a broken ceiling glass,
My life was shattered,
I was deranged about the arrangement!

Why do I need a scarf mask on my face?
Why do I need to tie a knot?
Knotting my bold tie to school?
I became a bride ahead of time.

Like a Jesus abnegated by Peter,
I was denied basic rights to childhood,
A wrapper of plight around my tiny waistline at night,
After my dowry was taken,
They said: "I was a burden".

Gifted to a partner enough to be a father,
They burnt down my bridges,
And left me alone on other side with this monster!
Facing life's realities too early.

The hit was hard,
At a drop of speech of my mind,
I became a sex doll,
My virginity wept!
Ahead of time I was a mother.
Singing songs of sorrow,
My life diary as ready lyrics,
A child backs a child,
My parents, society and hardship
Driven by the doctrine, led me to this,
I became a bride ahead of my time.

TRAUMA OF THE PIERCE

Uncle!
You said I should bring-forth my assignment,
And to stop being playful after school,
Why is my gown up? Is that what you meant?

You brought out gold circle,
But the topic is not shaped.
You covered my mouth, to mute trouble,
And wear the balloon for your long black ape.

You drilled my wall of Jericho,
And the Red Sea was flowing through my leg,
In pain like injured dealers of Mexico,
My virginity is shattered like a broken egg.

You gave me chocolate sweet in restrain,
To wipe off the sorrowful tears in my eyes,
You bought me a teddy bear to bear the pain.
Oh uncle, why? Why the lies?

Heavy wave of sadness storms my fragile mind,
Rain of bitterness fell on my sweet childhood,
Soaked in pool of blood after losing my pride,
Genesis of life, filled with touching memories!

BEHIND SHADOW OF RAPE

She shielded my shot and tied
Me up with her dancing tongue.
What have I done wrong?
Is it a crime to shoot a shot?
And pour the ocean of my feelings out at first?

Oh! My God!
I only showered you sweet words!
You kicked the bouquet of flower, right?
You don't want me?
Fine!
Can I just walk off in peace?
Without becoming a prisoner of love?

We made love with your consent,
No struggle, devoid of hitches,
You journey on the road of my intention,
My motive was clear; no police
How did we get here?
Is it because dove of our love is dead?
And post-breakfast is never peaceful?

Can you just imbibe it?
The faithful wine of rejection,
Just move on!
Why the stone of false accusations
Pelted at my glass house?

Your gender of loaded empathy!
Is it a crime to have a third leg?
Oh jury! I am not guilty....
My lord, please listen to me!
I am not guilty...

Oh ye society of humans!
I speak from deep sea of tears;
The one I am thrown into!
Crucify all false accusers,
Like you nailed the rapist,
Justice for one, justice for all,
Dead, the menace of rape,
Perish, the culture of false accusations.

NATION WITH NO DESTINATION

Nigeria, our ancestral land,
A kiss of my feat
- made me feel like a stranger,
Nigeria, the fertile land;
Hellish drought to soil farmers.

Oh ye ancestors of man!
Why sleep and slumber?
Oh ye master planner!
Is our land not in your plan?

Where are we going?
Judges with injustice,
Where are we going?
Doctors are sick.

Where are we going?
Preacher men fights and preach peace,
They paint tradition black and dirty,
Inflicting doses of disunity.
Oh my Nigeria!
Where are we going now?

Teachers fail crèche exams,
Knowledge cheapjack ignorance.
Where are we going, young lads?
For how long? For how far?

Immorality in mother's tone of ours,
Bedbug sucking our tomorrow tonight,
Looters built mansions in Freetown,
Patriots lives behind bar for years.

Independence! Independence!!
Yet, we depend on the source of our chain,
On the shoulder of law we rest,
Your treasonable laws…why bend to influences?

If only radio cast broadly the truths,
Without being scowled,
And freely like grass, Media freedom grows.

Giant ant of African nations!
Corrupt watchdog for corruption,
Nigeria my nation; drivers our dreams,
Where then is our destination?

UNITY IN DIVERSITY

The Marriage of 1914;
Maybe right, or wrong the thing,
- Has never been blissful,
Lake of our home is neither peaceful.

Our past heroes cried past,
Seeing the tug of war lasts,
"Stop! Stop!!" they yelled at us,
As politics dishes food of hatred to us.

Bring an African mother to price it,
Non-negotiable remains our Unity,
The reality we must begin to swallow,
Like the kola of bigotry we chewed low.

Like a goat bullying an hen in incinerators,
I hope we chase away the instigators;
The belly sitting with the national cake,
Let's dine together, to take their place.

MUSIC IS LIFE

Sad spider built webs
That curbed my heart,
When I lost wheel of my mind,
Fragile grievance
Weighed down my huge big body mass.

My sword and gun
Couldn't venture into the battle,
Only Bazooka of music hits differently,
The beat beats
And made me so losable!
My soul travelled unconsciously.

High spirit of music!
The base and treble
Wrestle the jinn of my worries,
And the dove of lyrics
Preaches the peace I seek,
Oh I am lost!
In the rhythm like unknown land!

I breathe via my playlist;
Every track is tied to my life!
In my rough times
It smoothens my soul,
Music indeed is life.

THE THESPIANS

Mountain of words,
From tumor world of cavemen,
Fold in ambit of thy head
And called the "script"
Cooked, then tasted by mankind.

Tragedians feed audience laughter of food,
Crying in realm of happiness thereafter,
The barnstormer journeys in lane of our emotion,
Oh!
The allusion of their rare creation.

Who are those behind the mask?
Crawling out of an overture ark?
Trafficking monologue paving way,
As they glow in the alligator costume array.

Dead souls but the stage breathes on us
Awakening the slumbering boredom in us,
We found the world on stage,
Watching the realities foretold by our sages.

The dance electrocuted legs,
The mummer in means and ends,
Where the casts visit home of our attention.

Oh I see!
These are thespians of creative vision.

The flame of their faceless stage
Aided our cold world to this age,
The climax that judged our conscience
In court of entertainment camera lens.
Oh! Oh!!

This is more than an act
But an art sustaining the societal pact.
Respect a thespian today!
Theatre is bailing us from eternal jail.

BEYOND THE PALMWINE

The cultured smoke of our culture
Fading away in the air of civilization's rapture.
Beyond the palm wine, is the brewed learned people?
Preserving Afro-norms in Social Thermocool.

The broken nation we lived in envies the glittering bamboo.
One who boos away
The gospel of "divide and rule"
Beyond the palm wine, is unity in diversity.
Where joyous guests preside on the podium of dichotomy.

Is it the shrine at the heart of higher institution?
Where few gather, like hives of bees for gyration.
Yes, you may be lost in wonder.
That the voice of the drum is armless,
Yet it draws passers-by to the circle of happiness.

Is it the chief at the palace of enjoyment
That sends burdens into exile?
Where Suicide cried and was shamed,
For only happy souls will rise to fame?

Even the blind have seen their peaceful war,
Rebelling against social-vices.
Where cultism maintains social distance.
Beyond the hairy staff in the air,
Is it the air of humanity?
They breathe into the campus atmosphere.

The deaf wall could hear clearly.
The sounding legacy of Fatomilola
Mapping out for the blind:
The proud path of Soyinka.
I say unto thee, verily, I say unto thee.
Beyond the palm wine drinkards' club
Is a Kegite of cultured Notables.

OJUDE OBA

If the Earth was made theirs,
Like the fore-court of Awujale,
Watch them spread their Agemo's mats,
And group human into regberegbe.

Ojude Oba - the day of beautiful surprises,
When economists rove in deep water of money,
Mock war and rising anxieties,
The palace bards drop bars of poetry.

The stallions wear a smile – flamboyantly
Ridden by offsprings of heroic Baloguns,
Their Dansiki armed – not violently
But with piercing gators of the Ojawus.

Cultural Attires could not be tired,
Getting displayed in colorful matches,
With Auras the Gbobaleye could not hide,
Stepping to Bata's rhythmic laces.

It is the Artistic Beauty or the heritage therein
Ojude Oba, astonishing Royal Fete
Projecting their culture to global screens,
A day eyes are fed and mouth can tell.

HEINOUS TRIBAL MARK

With a glowing face I came to your world,
Like other infants, on my first day, they rejoiced,
Talking drums talked love and welcoming,
Generosity at a glance, not the heinous forthcoming.

Betoken steps from my mother,
Like a criminal I was handed over to skin carver,
Wuan! Wuan!! Wuan!!! In state of acute pain I cried,
Suddenly, my face got stamped and lined.

In jiffy my cheek turned red like a fire deck,
Blood swims with tears flowing down my neck,
Like moon and stars I was close to death,
Where is the angel that brought me to earth?

The scar healed takes away my beauty,
Pure minded but the mirror says I am a beast,
I reflect behind the mud-wall and cried for justice,
Who shall show me tons of sympathies?

When tradition endorsed an act and calls it art,
God! Can you take me back to your path?
My self-esteem was down to ground,
Oh! What a lion fighter of zero grand!

This is madness of cultural trademark,
Indoor in daylight; "We are outside" only in the dark?
"For better for worse", my marriage of barbaric barrier!
It's sad, Time heals everything except a tribal mark.

CHRISTMAS NOT MERRY

Transients like day and night,
Quickly the merry fades off
Not the strings of hunger.
Herein, is platter of the street,
Where gold neither glitters
Nor shines like the sun of our hope
In shades of uncertainty.
Painful was the joy
- As the ants of our mouth
Swallow the giant elephant
Of your dining table.

Sitting with you leftovers;
We are your leftovers
Underneath your world's bridge
We live, homelessly.
Maybe, someday
In hope of a broken egg,
Our Christmas will be Merry
On the other side!

TABLE MANNER

Our Elysian Father,
Sitting as the most high,
We the graceful ones, see you not,
But clearly we sight your love
Even in dire times.

Not running like a horse,
Strong hulk? Never! We are not...
Like a Fox - some run than we do,
We are weak as a rat in a pool.

Bunch starves now,
Daylight for their plights
- Empty belle, all nights,
Are they cripple hustling tortoise nor bad?
Our inch above them is your grace
- That clouded our sky.

Some have food but cannot eat,
Some can eat but have no food to eat,
Gracefully, we have food
Joyfully, we can dine,
- Wholeheartedly, from table of gratitude.

JOURNEY OF COMMON DESTINATION

We journey with big muscle,
Age weaken the flex,
Even in shamble of disarray
Time cared less.

Some fly like eagles,
And glitter like peacocks,
In oily bag filled with able-ness,
Not the "time" -just the clock.

Whether smooth a journey or not,
White horse or cracked black foot,
Whether have or have not,
Diverse routes, same destination.

Death comes, takes the wheel
And map of life, Oceans of tears
Can't keep the poor alive,
The rich shall sleep forever, thinking it's a nap.

From birth to death,
Either happiness or commotion,
The hustle and bustle of long length,
Grave is everyone's destination.

GRAVE LOVE

With my grave flooded with tears,
My soul cried to rise above the pit
They laugh in the death ties,
And weep in my life arrears.

They watched me die naked
Wrap me up with yards of a golden attire,
They made me sleep forever with the dead,
And wish the dove of my soul didn't fly higher.

My stomach grumbles,
I died of hunger,
Sadly, ocean of food floods the tables,
At the coast of my funeral.

Why am I loved after death?
When spitted hatred in my lifetime?
You couldn't take step of half length,
But you walk miles in no time after my lifetime.

You broke the bank for my funeral,
But couldn't give a dime to keep me alive.
Life was critical and hypocritical,
Crocodile tears are waters of the living.

Bring the rose when am alive!
Show me love when I still breathe!
When death comes visiting,
Love after death; is a futile vanity.

IMOLE

Dazzling is the flame,
Like the candle of the day, rising to fame,
The star on a tour - even at noon,
To shine in sky with dark moons.

"I am the light, Imole!" he says to them,
And took to heart like Marlians Anthem,
But the industry Feels - no- Good, Oh I see!
His potentials - Plenty as the sand of the sea.

Sadly, an ambush of death came through,
Prayer couldn't pay the price and it slides,
Oh! Dear Mohbad,
We know you're not bad.

If the crusade of a second life comes alive,
And you thread your path back to life,
We hope you get to bench Ronaldo and Messi,
Till then - Imole be at Peace.

AFRIKA LIVES ON

Iwilade George "Afrika"
Murdered in a frowning massacre,
His soul saved in grave like pulse of death,
For OAU to be the arena safe on earth.

Oh! Comrade, raided with Oau'5,
Voices from wilderness shun cultism alive,
July 10 1999; peace broken into pieces
& your soul crave for justice like bee's honey.

Indeed a warrior with seldom valour,,
From thy struggle comet our freedom,
The messenger was killed, not the message,
Afrika is us, we are Afrika in sage.

Moon years today since your departure,
Forever in land of our heart with green pasture,
We shall live with the scar of your humanity,
And keep sailing in spirit of unity.

The clarion call of gods of Aluta we won't decline,
& on table of thy struggle we shall continue to dine,
Until we meet again in exile dear Afrika,
Aluta continua Victoria Ascerta.

GOD IS EVERYWHERE

On a sunny day I make hay,
While the sun shines and dresses up in haste,
I dust my bible and journey in book of Jeremiah,
A loud praise with my solo mouth; my desire.

Like a righteous gentile,
I see the Holy Spirit with closed eyes,
I preach to myself here,
'Cause God is everywhere.

I poured remnants of my sins away
And bad deeds, washed away,
God touched my heart at long run,
I worship my God, not the church nor religion.

"Judge not" God says!
Church is the mind not congregation of hypocrites,
Pray and praise him anywhere,
Verily, verily I say unto thee, God is everywhere.

THE AGUERO'S MOMENT

Just like a defeated Soldier,
My Heart dropped the gun
My mind hanged the boot
With the regalia of hustle and bustle.

I speak like a Veteran of Failure,
A futile hustler of the year,
So, I clean my sour sweat,
With my collar of hopelessness.

Delayed hope makes the heart sick -
Of course, I have to wrap it up,
And try again - maybe Next Year
But will never give up - not totally.

Until he pulled the stunt of deadline,
And resonated my dying Hope,
Oh yes! Kun Aguero! – He did it,
For God is not dead, so believe it!

MY MOREMÍ ÀJÀSORÒ

With an empty heart
- a place for my best-part,
Merging empty stomach I had,
 For the breakfasts I was served.

The sneer to my love life,
And hope in your high five,
Your smile and beauty
- Promising an eternity.

Let my worries be carted away,
I hope even in my disarray,
You will fight by my side,
And never let your promises slide

LOVE PRICE

I sat down in hell,
Building life of comfort.
Can I yell?
No! I fought and no one to fault,
My soul left,
My heart wept,
Like nothing left
In my vessel of sacrifice,
Oh!
Nothing to rip.
I gave my all.
Paid the price with my last sweat.
Big court and no ball!
Oh price of love!
Mind of wealth got drained,
I am finished,
Back to jungle of singles.
Even when I braced the falling of building,
Aftermath of love was sour,
Leaving my back shattered.

BE LIKE ZAINAB

Nab with the hands of your beauty;
A glucose guardian to guide with,
Draw closer with your Gen-z strings,
One that sharpens only in 20's.

Feed craving hungry eyes
- Of Social Media, with true lies,
Win clicks when your plan clicks,
And leave in trashcan - your cliques.

Let Ajala-Traveler envy from heaven,
As you fly in the sky for moon,
Grass is greener on Alhaji's side,
The Elon of the mosque in lakeside.

Like a reigning baddie,
Enjoy the throne but never be ready,
To tie the knot even if he's nuts;
Will you be like Zainab or not?

SONNET FROM MY HEART

She is a unique Sugar,
Walks like waves of sea salt,
Her fluffy white teeth are like strings,
Of dancing fingers on guitar,
Blowing beats of love,
Making hearts of ant-men beat
- And running to have a taste of her beauty,
She walks majestically,
To the only empty room of my heart,
Like a dove finding shelter in the rain,
She's my peace: so I am to her,
My heart a resort,
And her heart my only harmony,
The bond is unbreakable.

KOPA WAA KOPA WEE-MEN

Who will tell the rat on a dance-stage?
That its home is for the hunting Cat?
That watches from owl's window range,
Entertained to their cart's fill.

If hell is light
With a dazzling flame,
Like the lamp of Africans' night,
His Pen will not be tamed.

Let the border of love be closed,
When the Nation is short of words,
All will be kept 'em stallions close;
To worship him high than their lords.

Maybe, it's a theory in politics;
With their Jaws down the hills,
His game and the tricks;
A veteran of E-struggle - we miss.

WEATHER FOR TWO

As the cloud journeys by,
It takes rest at the sky's stopover,
Whose blue layers send an army of breezes,
Dancing around the earth with ease.

Whenever heaven's reservoir leaks,
Nature takes a shower - yes! It rains.
My generation gets wet under their roofs,
And weather for two is approved.

Ladies jump on motorcycle yachts,
Crossing the borders of streets without let,
Boys marry their windows' frames,
Hoping for complimentary arrivals.

Cottons down, doors shut, lights out!
Sound system's base breaks into the walls,
The rhythm of blues and Afro beats dominate,
& moans behind the scene gravitates.

From the comfort of my bed, I feel the circle,
I cuddle my pillow, wondering the doings of Singles,
Though horny, never will I sour my soul,
Verify! Verily!! Heaven is my goal.

THE BODY COUNT COUNTS

Heavy toes walk unholy tiptoes
On a Pilgrimage to her Body,
Like the road to Mecca,
Giving free pass for men in-to her.

A bad goalie she is in her noon,
Every shot leaves her legs open,
In her NGO of squirt and cream,
Running charity of Hits to brim.

"The count doesn't count" she says,
Hoping blazing suit man will surface,
Hoping Akanji will suit her well,
The one-eyed boy on love's spell.

Blinded to her dirty pasts in the shower,
Unclean-able with rose flower,
Truly: the body count counts,
Be all, but the last – On her census count.

TRAUMA OF MASTURBATION

The girl's b*tt is bigger than the universe,
Enough to make walking dead men reverse,
Oh! The bre*st, it seems large,
But, men's love for her ends in mirage.

Everyone in a relationship,
But she's happily sad with herself-situationship.
Cucumber is picked over pick-men's of men,
Saying "s*x toys never cheats like men".

"Men are scum." She says,
And dance with her cl*toris in hidden ways,
P*rnography: the image in her soul
Oh! She ripped the pleasure she sow!

Men made the lotion company smile,
And, the Vaseline seller grew a long mile,
P*rn hubs entertain when they visit.
They jerk off and never admit.

Masturbation oh masturbation!
Ladies and gents, all homeless in your mansion
Masturbation; One that paints image of lust.
In your land of addiction everyone gets lost.

Hey you masturbation!

Let your ears bleed,
Because souls are crying as the heart pleads,
Loneliness becomes a priority.
Indeed a monster in close door, oh what a pity!

It drains all my energies,
I just want to get over this!
The thoughts flow like a river in my head,
"Free me!" I scream every day in my head.

Oh ye! Ladies and gents, mingle to kill boredom,
Let your mind walk in all paths to freedom,
Masturbation is armless but it kills silently,
End it now! Soon, it will end you loudly.

SILHOUETTE IN THE DARK

Jumped on the trend
Between door frames, end to end,
Blinking red light, shining bright
Like stars of the night.

Dress down in jiffy,
Conscience buried in bold cemetery,
Everything looks normal,
Darkness descends from hell and goes viral.

Tities are up
Causing Goosebumps,
Twisting like serpent
Hands on shoulders like the devil's arrest.

Lust in bittersweet way,
Seduction and deception in unusual way,
Oh no! It stops loading...
Oceans of data refilled like you refuelling.

Ladies become obsessed
- Guys became possessed,
Immoralities in new version,
"All for fun" says their action.

Trends of Challenge it is,
Blinded to future unborn challenges,
Souls were sold to the devil,
Illuminating evil ways.

Oh! My generation…
My tears for Thee floods the whole nation,
Dignity rolled in mud of pleasure,
My pen speaks to secure a sane future.

THE UNPRIVILEGED GRADUATE

I am Uche from the heart of Niger Delta,
A brother to Adisa of Sango-Ota
My friend is Aminu from Sokoto
Who shall we children of the poor, run to?

We never tasted death but we are born again,
Our parents lack all but their offerings retain,
The altar lives in the Jerusalem of the minds
& Their Mecca is precious like apple of their eyes.

Eh Ehn…
Hon. Aliu is dead to our cries,
Sadly, Gov. Keshinro's mouth is a tunnel of lies,
How then shall President Eze hear us
When their dining table is placed upon us?

Who then shall we run to brothers & brethren?
The costly education of now was free then.
Oh!
The elites are building their Jericho,
Education is forbidden but not for rich fellows.

The preachers are building varsities,
Unaffordable to the holy poor boy in the city.
Yes!

Our parents' tithes: the brick of their foundation,
"Religion is opium of the masses" says the revelation.

Who shall we run to in the nation,
When they marginalized the poor from education,
Our dream in the slum is to wear the khaki,
And not smile in squalid camp of Almanjiri?

Education they say is the best legacy,
But they jail us behind the bar of illiteracy.
We're pregnant with the dying hope of a better future,
We are the unprivileged graduates that you nurture.

THE DAY IN GOWN

The patched head;
The shattered heart.
The fainted hope water couldn't wake,
The injuries sustained when JAMB jammed.

The monitor frowns,
- And keyboard itches.
The score I couldn't score
Even at the wide open net of EXPO.

When jammed by casualties of JAMB;
My re-applying bone got broken.
My epidemic POST-UME score,
That makes all "choices" rejects me.

The insults, kitchen's plates' showers on me,
The alarm of shrinking bad eyes from my parents,
Reminds me of how much older I am growing,
That makes the sweet dinner got bitter and sour.

Oh!
Finally! Finally!!
Here I am,
In a campus of academics heaven.

Tomorrow is tomorrow!
The tortoise of my anxiety, in spirit of a fox.
My soul travels to lands of imagination.
I can't wait.
I can't wait to see the colorful day,
—my heart longs for you,
The day in gown.

Hey tomorrow!
Can you just stop running?
You're getting too far indeed.
I can't just wait,
For the day to be in gown.

SCHOOL GATE FOREST

The dusk is down
On it kneels,
The pen has been dropped
With dripping sweat,
"It's a wrap" says the hand
That craves A-Four paper
- A present of degree.

The moon was stressed out
Quickly than we thought,
Dawn came with a long drooling,
Everyone is awake to reality
Of life, behind the learning wall,
"Who is to lean on?"
The hunters asked...

Some are bearing double barrels,
Some with half-baked gunpowder,
The hot heads;
Are with voodoo ribbons,
And a fat trigger-thirsty guard,
Everyone is armed accordingly.

The parade, the marches, the chants,
Heavy at the Country square,
The hunters depart
And set out at sunrise,
Towards the school gate Forest,
What is their fate?
That, I cannot answer.

Everyone scampered for elephants,
Like a pressed cap
Is enough to pull it down,
In the forest of squirrels?
Laughable is the faith,
Maybe laughable, or not,
The hunters continue to hunt,
In hope
That their hope won't haunt.

STIFLE THE SUICIDE

Keep the momentum
That of shackles and struggles
Slum you came from?
Yes!
The world on your fragile head?
Life kisses you with lips laced with bitterness?
Life seems worthless?

Wait there!
Hang in there!

The dark days in world of light?
You sober on your sofa?
The nights, the universe goes deaf
- With your cries?
But no one hears, Oh!

You mean the unmovable awful days
That feels like forever?
When you find no joy in no lullaby,
And you walk round the earth in angle of your room.

Wait!
Hang in there!

See the unborn days with your eyes closed,
Where to-day exists only in book of calendar,
Let the mind give the soul a hand,
Lift the soul with all you see,
- and the head up above the sky.

See it!
See the smoke fading away
Like cloud of growing morning,
Oh yes!
That's the bad days walking into exile,
See the sun smiling?
Full of transition you never see,
Don't end it yet,
Light will shine on you soon!

BEHIND THE "HAPPY FAMILY

The glittering ring has spoken like a dragon
Splashing the testimony of sworn vows.
Behind the "happy family";
Lies "For better for worse".

An oath of sad and happy people,
Like the communion of the demons.
The eyes are crying to have a mouth,
Grieving at the dead voice of the mouth.

One who couldn't say a drop
Of the ocean of pains the eyes sees?
Boom! The thoughts of eyes became so loud:
"Oh Yeh mouth! Why burying the pains in the morgue of happiness?"
"Happy family"; the mask of joy on the face of their sorrow.

Behind the "happy family",
Lies the days of party of brokenness,
When the hungry belly feeds on hope,
And the bread winner got defeated.

Behind the "happy family"
Lies the union that ends with the gown and suit,
And the smiles that exist only on wall of sitting room;
The memories of good that fails to fall from the photo frame.

Is it the domestic wild violence
Where the rain of punches leaked their roof?
And the wedlock became a prison,
Behind the "happy family" is the union of tears.

Who then shall be voice of the pain?
And narrates how the crown was wore on leg.
Who then shall open the dam of tears of madam?
"For better for worse"; the chain of the freedom!

Here comes the battlefield of love,
Where the street is slippery and forbidden.
No going back!
Neither leave nor transfer!
Where endurance becomes the commander,
Like the point of no return.

Behind the "happy family".
Where colorful wedding handover
To the colorless marriage.
Where "For better for worse" presides.
In the realm of your soliloquy,
Are you indeed ready
For the scenes behind the happy family?
Truly the grass is not greener on the other side.

PODIUM OF ANXIETY

Like a desert, the land is tasty,
Waiting to drink from the sea of my word,
The stage is wailing
For the lullaby of my knowledge.

The sound of claps command,
Making the atmosphere bow like a tree in the wind,
Friends & lovers waiting like coming of savior,
With earth of expectations rotating in their heart.

Oh!
I was overwhelmed
& effortlessly fight the war within,
Sadly, the stage fright fought me high,
The mic was deaf to my weeping thoughts begging to be said.

My voice was cracking without an earthquake
My soul was helpless as words flee from me,
& My self-esteem was drowning on a hill.

Oh!
What a bad good day
With a show of demotivation!
"Head up!
It's a step to a journey of greatness
A path of failure to the point of success"

 Says my instinct.

I learn and unlearn in the podium of anxiety.

TALIBANS AT OUR BACKYARD

They feed on blood and festers,
Remember the Jos of years back?
- When church programs
End without sharing the grace?

Remember the Salah that scattered
When bodies split around like Salah meat?
The suicide bombers,
The genocides of "Niger Area"?
Those we nurse with our mediocrity and hypocrisy?
Remember the deaths we sponsored
While promising heaven and earth?
Remember the shield we gave them
- And those who shot at us in war?

Remember the ethnic card
That outplayed justice?
Remember the religious agenda
That makes up the law?
Remember the death
We pet and called "repent"?
Yes! They are here! They are coming,
The little birds we once kept in our Next
Are now bigger than dinosaurs.

Their wings cover our earth
And the sun can't even breathe.
They are here!
In different species but same root
And same forest.
Some are unknown gunmen!
Some are known gunmen –
Some are armed uniform men!
Yes! They are much in our sky
Like pimples of the cloud,
They prey on us like vultures do,
The white of our flag is now red,
Our land is crying and sobering for help.

Those we granted amnesty,
Cripple the efforts of gallant patriots.
Yes! They are the havoc of our architecture.
Our craft that is casting our coffin.

Insurgents are here - Insurgents are coming
Coming to rape the constitution
And guide us with GUN-stitution.
The courageous uniform men will flee.
Those in agbada will fly Jerichos.

They are here!
The TALIBANS at our backyard.

SIX NINE

Cloud sat in the sky,
The rain of words –
That of five wig men everyone craves,
The Konji of justice!

Parties are throwing a party of petitions,
Air refreshed - bed spread in haste,
To move into the Villa,
All eyes through the window.

Watching and waiting
- Arrival of beauty of judiciary,
A dream dead on arrival,
Justice seized to cum.

The third leg never rises,
Second man puts in six positions
- For nine minutes,
The conspiracy lasted too soon.

Wrap it up, Oh ye Saints!
Democracy has been raped,
Neither today, nor yesterday,
Hope in the system has passed out.

SNAKES ON LEGAL TENDER

I understand the tenderable currency
- Of our giant tempered country
Is scarce like a well in the desert,
Our pocket has no cash drink, beyond alert.

I see with blind eyes of no doubt,
Your struggle for it, in lion's mouth,
I mean the salty sweat you donate
To Emefiele's ocean of ego.

I understand your spot is spotted on,
Then, you became a bitter sugar icon,
Where ants of suffering single out people,
Searching for Note-rallies around you.

But to that Pest like P.O.S agent,
Who sees the pressuring moment?
To leisure and climb to top of FOBES,
Time will turn on you soon, beyond this time.

THE HEN THE ROPE

Ukraine - Russia
Finds home...
In the farm of our dining table,
Feeding becomes war,
Yes, numbers are agrieved,
But not many are fuming
- With the Villa,
And its white fabric spider-men,
The shepherds of zombies,
In the map with natural groceries,
Cry not for the bereaved,
  - They are known survivors,
  Crashed in a clash of Amnesia..
The Hen perches on the rope
- Neither the Hen nor the rope,
Shall be at peace.

THE MESSENGER OF OUR PLIGHTS

"Shut the parrot!
The wailing patriot
The voice of their dead we hide,
The Lazarus of their dead mind.

Set the wings ablaze,
The carrier of our bad in haste,
Lock up the beak,
That breathes our wrong to public.

Raze down their blue community
The shelter for their advocacy.
Blind the eyes of the bird App they had
& the voice of their yelling keypad.

Jack down the App of Mr Elon-Jack.
The space revealing our dark.
Shut them up with the power lock"
Says the "oppressors" at Aso rock.

I can hear birds sing
From the grave of victims.
"You can kill the prophet, but not the prophecy"
The soul of our heroes beg for mercy.

Tweet from the tree of their Rome,
The blue App is our home,
The echo of our cracking voices,
Keep it on & nothing shall discourage us.

AUTHORIZED CRIMINALS

The black armed men on black are bad,
Killing young lads,
Cause they aren't looking tattered,
Paid from our sweat to chase us to sweat.

The hardworking lads in their prime,
Muscles stretch for legal crafts at all times,
Weeping sour tears like lime.
Is looking good a crime?

Security men render us insecure,
Brutality like pandemic of no cure,
The dirty men arresting the pure,
Show your ID and they get it torn.

End SARS now, don't ask how!
Future leaders are dying like fowls
You speak and they move you like cow,
Rise and roar, make SARS to bow.

THE KIDNEY OF THE COUNTRY

Waking up daily in my country,
The Eagles on our Coat of Arms whispers to me;
Why this Nation?
Where the poor wants to get rich,
Faster on motion of greediness.

Why are the entrepreneurs creative?
Investing and striving in Techno-Death industry,
Then I bruise my teeth with chemical of Open Up
- That I thought was Close up,
I was shocked and couldn't close my Mouth.

I walked into the Nightlife, where we equally lose lives,
I saw the rich Man's pikin oppressing
- And intimidating the Poor man's pikin,
Putting light on Casket, dorimeee!!
And paying hugely for their own Caskets,
Popping Champagne from the Brewery in bungalows of Agege.

I burst into Tears, assisting the cry of our livers
- At the Funeral of our Kidneys,
Wrap it up Nigaa!
I had to stopped quickly
'cause I didn't want to get sick from Mourning,
As the drugs in Pharmacy are deadlier than sniper.

Oh dear NAFDAC!
I mean the Original men on red jacket,
Look at us!
We failed to produce chemical weapons,
But the people are falling and dying
On the streets like its Chinese Flu.

This is our own Tsunami,
The original fake we are consuming
- is digging our grave so early.

The Country is on fire,
And sadly, no original water to quench it,
Before it ends us, we must rise to end
And the business men behind the cottons.

MAN' UNITED

To the folks of Trafford,
My watery eyes could see the fire,
As the red devil was bullied at the end,
Oh! The devil pleaded.

From a distance I heard sea waves of tears,
From your thousand eyes. What a faded red!
Penalty your escape route in cold,
Yet, you end up in sunny ambush road.

Sleeping Red Devils of Manchester,
How long shall your people suffer?
Once a king in island of champions,
Now a servant, so distant to cups.

Air your hope to err depression,
Let your devil pray to God against relegation,
Hope not for what will never come,
For this trying time shall stay so long.

ADISA THE TAILOR

Your mouth was sweet,
Leaving my doubt with diabetics.
You promised to deliver
- with a piercing gator.
But days ride on days like horses.

And the day comes knocking on my door
Oh! Adisa the London tailor
I'm here to live on dying minutes,
Say some new words Adisa.

The encyclopedia of your lies
"we outside" my mind says;
"No ankara no semo" my body laments.
What then shall I say to Simbi my love?
Waiting at the heart of the road?

Should my day be beheaded,
Coming back is forbidden you know,
Sew my drip or I take your soul Adisa
Certainly one must drip today,
Either your head or my body.

www.ingramcontent.com/pod-product-compliance
Lightning Source LLC
Chambersburg PA
CBHW060034180426
43196CB00045B/2675